Printed in China

Distributed By:

507 Industrial Street
Waverly, IA 50677

ISBN-13: 978-1-56383-495-0

You're gonna love these no-bake bars, cookies, cakes, and desserts.

A few tips:

1 Line your pans with parchment paper, waxed paper, plastic wrap, or foil and then coat with cooking spray if you'd like to help keep the pan clean and make removing the treats a snap. When it's time to cut, simply lift treats by the ends of the wrap and set the whole thing on a cutting board.

2 Use fresh ingredients for the best results.

3 To cut sticky bars and desserts, use a sharp knife that has been coated with cooking spray or dipped into hot water and dried with a towel.

4 For a sharp, even cut, push the point of your knife down through the bar or dessert completely at the corner and then make your cut.

5 Serving sizes are based on personal preference. Cut more or fewer pieces as desired to make the serving size fit your needs.

Nothin' says lovin' like No Oven Lovin'!

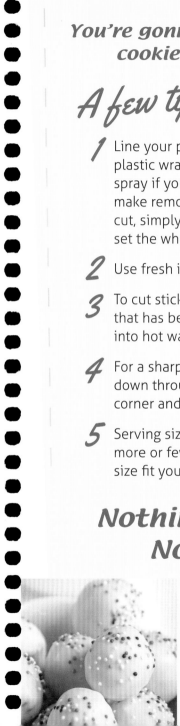  

Gooey Chocolate-Butterscotch Treats

makes 32

you'll need

6 T. butter, melted

1 C. creamy peanut butter

1½ C. powdered sugar

1 (9 oz.) pkg. chocolate wafers, crushed

1 (11 oz.) pkg. butterscotch chips

¼ C. heavy cream

¾ C. coarsely chopped salted dry roasted peanuts

In a large bowl, stir together butter, peanut butter, and powdered sugar until well mixed. Stir in the wafer crumbs. Press mixture evenly into an ungreased 9 x 13" pan; set aside.

In a medium bowl, microwave butterscotch chips and cream until melted, stirring until smooth. Spread mixture over chocolate layer in pan. Sprinkle with peanuts, pressing down gently.

Chill until set before cutting.

Helpful Hint: Pop them in the freezer to cut chill time in half.

Vanilla-Fudge Bars

you'll need

makes 48

- 1 C. sugar
- 1 C. light corn syrup
- 2 C. peanut butter
- 3 C. each Rice Krispies and Corn Flakes cereals
- ¾ C. plus ½ C. butter, divided
- 4 C. powdered sugar
- 2 (3.4 oz.) pkgs. vanilla instant pudding
- ¼ to ½ C. milk
- 1 (12 oz.) pkg. milk chocolate chips
- Unsalted chopped peanuts

Line a 10 x 15" pan with foil, letting foil extend over edges; set aside.

In a large saucepan over medium heat, combine sugar and syrup. Heat until the mixture just begins to boil; cook for 1 minute more, stirring constantly. Remove from heat and add the peanut butter, stirring until melted and smooth. Stir in both cereals until well coated. Press mixture evenly into prepared pan and set aside.

In a large bowl, microwave ¾ cup butter until melted. Stir in powdered sugar, pudding, and ¼ cup milk until well blended, adding more milk if needed for spreading consistency. Spread evenly over cereal mixture; set aside.

In a separate bowl, heat remaining ½ cup butter and chocolate chips in the microwave until melted. Pour over pudding mixture and spread to cover. Sprinkle with the peanuts.

Chill until set before cutting.

makes 24

Let's Jam
Cheesecake Bars

you'll need

- 2 C. cinnamon graham cracker crumbs
- ½ C. butter, melted
- ¼ C. sugar
- 4 (8 oz.) pkgs. cream cheese, softened
- 3 C. powdered sugar, sifted
- ½ C. strawberry preserves (or flavor of your choice)
- 2½ C. chopped fresh strawberries (or fruit of your choice)
- 1 (8 oz.) tub whipped topping, thawed

to make

In a 9 x 13" pan, stir together cracker crumbs, butter, and sugar until well blended. Press firmly into pan and chill.

In a large bowl, beat cream cheese until smooth. Slowly beat in powdered sugar. Stir in preserves and berries; fold in whipped topping and spread evenly over crust.

Chill several hours before cutting. Garnish with strawberries, if you'd like.

Black Forest Sprial Cream Cake

serves 16

you'll need

16 cream-filled chocolate cake rolls (such as Swiss Rolls)

⅓ C. cherry preserves

12 oz. cream cheese, softened

½ C. powdered sugar

1 tsp. clear vanilla

¾ C. heavy cream

Bittersweet or dark chocolate shavings

Arrange four cake rolls side by side across the width of a serving plate, long sides touching. Position four more cake rolls on the plate with their short ends touching the short ends of the previous rolls. Spread preserves evenly over the eight rolls. Arrange a second layer of eight rolls directly on top; gently push on all four sides to align. Freeze for 1 hour or until preserves have hardened slightly.

In a medium bowl, beat cream cheese, powdered sugar, and vanilla until smooth and creamy. Slowly add cream, beating until mixture is thick and spreadable. Spread mixture evenly over top and sides of chilled cake. Sprinkle with chocolate shavings.

Refrigerate several hours before cutting.

Helpful Hint: Make chocolate shavings by running a vegetable peeler against the edge of a chocolate bar.

Rainbow Treats

makes 9

you'll need

- ¼ C. butter
- 4 C. mini marshmallows
- 1 C. salted peanuts
- 3 C. each Cheerios and Trix cereals

Coat a 9 x 9" pan with cooking spray; set aside.

In a large saucepan, melt the butter. Add the marshmallows and cook until melted, stirring constantly. Remove from heat. Add peanuts and both cereals, stirring until well coated. Transfer mixture to prepared pan and press into an even layer.

Set aside to cool before cutting.

Helpful Hint: Coating the back of a large spoon with cooking spray works well when pressing cereal mixture into pan.

makes 32

Cookie Dough Bars

you'll need

3¼ C. milk chocolate chips, divided

½ C. creamy peanut butter, divided

1 C. butter, softened, divided

½ C. sugar

¼ C. milk

1 (7 oz.) container marshmallow creme

2½ tsp. clear vanilla, divided

1 C. coarsely chopped, salted dry roasted peanuts

1 (14 oz.) pkg. caramels

¼ C. plus 2 T. heavy cream, divided

⅔ C. brown sugar

1 C. flour

¼ tsp. salt

⅔ C. mini chocolate chips

1 C. pretzel sticks

to make

Heavily grease a 9 x 13" pan; set aside.

Melt together 1¼ cups milk chocolate chips and ¼ cup peanut butter; pour into prepared pan, spreading evenly. Place in freezer for 15 minutes.

In a medium saucepan, melt ¼ cup butter over medium heat. Stir in sugar and milk; bring to a boil and cook for 5 minutes, stirring occasionally. Add marshmallow creme and 1 teaspoon vanilla, stirring until smooth. Remove from heat and stir in peanuts; set aside for 5 minutes then pour over chocolate layer, spreading evenly. Chill for 15 minutes.

Unwrap caramels and melt together with ¼ cup cream in a double boiler, stirring until smooth. Quickly pour over marshmallow layer, spreading carefully to cover. Chill for 15 minutes.

In a medium bowl, beat remaining ¾ cup butter, brown sugar, remaining 2 tablespoons cream, and remaining 1½ teaspoons vanilla until fluffy. Beat in flour and salt to combine. Stir in mini chocolate chips; spread over caramel layer.

Melt together 1½ cups milk chocolate chips and remaining ¼ cup peanut butter; drizzle evenly over creamy layer, spreading to cover. Arrange pretzels on top. Melt remaining ½ cup milk chocolate chips and drizzle over pretzels.

Chill at least 1 hour before cutting.

serves 24

M&M
Popcorn Cake

you'll need

- 2 (3.2 oz.) pkgs. microwave butter-flavored popcorn
- 2 C. salted dry roasted peanuts
- 1½ C. plain M&Ms
- ½ C. butter
- 1 (16 oz.) pkg. mini marshmallows

to make

Coat an angel food cake pan with cooking spray; set aside. Pop popcorn and dump it into a very large bowl, removing unpopped kernels. Stir in peanuts and M&Ms. Set all aside.

In a large bowl, melt butter in the microwave. Stir in the marshmallows and microwave until puffed. Stir until smooth and melted; let set for 2 minutes. Pour marshmallow mixture over popcorn mixture and stir to coat evenly. Press mixture into prepared pan. Cover and let set 1 hour.

Run a knife between popcorn mixture and pan to loosen cake. Place a serving plate upside down over the top and invert pan to remove cake before cutting.

Helpful Hint: *Since the popcorn mixture is sticky, putting your hand inside a plastic bag while pressing the popcorn into the pan works great!*

Saucepan Date Balls

In a saucepan, melt ½ C. butter; mix in 1 C. sugar and 1 C. chopped dates. Cook and stir for 4 minutes. Put ¼ cup egg substitute into a small bowl; add a bit of the hot mixture and stir to blend. Return to pan, beating until well blended. Remove from heat; stir in 1 tsp. vanilla and 2¼ C. Rice Krispies cereal. Drop by tablespoonful into powdered sugar; shake to coat then shape into balls. Set on waxed paper until firm.

makes 20

Hazelnut Sprinkles

In a saucepan, heat together ½ C. butter, 2 C. sugar, and ⅔ C. hazelnut-flavored liquid coffee creamer until smooth and melted. Boil for 1 minute, stirring constantly. Stir in ½ tsp. each vanilla and almond extract, ½ C. sliced almonds, and 3 C. quick-cooking oats. Cook and stir 1 minute more. Remove from heat; let set a few minutes then stir in ¼ C. jumbo nonpareils. Drop by heaping tablespoonful onto waxed paper. Let set until firm.

makes 40

Choco-Cherry Bites

Microwave 1 C. semi-sweet chocolate chips and ¾ C. white baking chips until melted; stir until smooth. Stir in 1½ C. Rice Krispies cereal, ¾ C. coarsely chopped dried cherries, ⅓ C. slivered almonds, and ½ tsp. vanilla. Drop by tablespoonful onto waxed paper. Let set until firm.

makes 20

Malted Milk Drops

In a saucepan, heat together ½ C. butter, 2 C. sugar, ¼ C. unsweetened cocoa powder, 1 T. malt powder, ½ C. chocolate milk, ¼ tsp. salt, and 1 T. vanilla until melted and smooth, stirring often. Bring to a boil; boil and stir for 1 minute. Remove from heat; stir in 1 C. creamy peanut butter, 2 C. quick-cooking oats, and 1 C. coconut. Drop by tablespoonful onto waxed paper; top with Almond Joy Pieces or crushed malted milk balls. Let set until firm.

makes 36

Microwave Scotcheroos

serves 12

you'll need

- 1 C. light corn syrup
- 1 C. sugar
- 1 C. crunchy peanut butter
- 1 tsp. vanilla
- 6 C. Rice Krispies cereal
- 1 C. semi-sweet chocolate chips
- 1½ C. butterscotch chips

Coat a 9 x 13" pan with cooking spray; set aside.

In a large bowl, microwave syrup and sugar together until mixture boils. Stir in peanut butter and vanilla until blended. Add cereal, stirring until well coated. Spread evenly in prepared pan.

Melt together chocolate and butterscotch chips; stir until smooth. Spread evenly over the top of the cereal mixture. Chill until set.

Let set at room temperature 15 to 20 minutes before cutting.

Coconut-Pecan Jumbles

you'll need

About 17 whole graham crackers, divided

1 egg

½ C. milk

¾ C. butter

1 C. sugar

1 C. graham cracker crumbs

1 C. chopped pecans

1 C. shredded coconut

1 (16 oz.) tub cream cheese frosting

Coat a 9 x 13" pan with cooking spray and line the bottom with graham crackers, cutting as needed; set aside.

In a bowl, beat together egg and milk. In a large saucepan, melt butter; stir in sugar. Slowly whisk egg mixture into butter mixture. Continue whisking until mixture comes to a boil. Remove from heat. Stir in cracker crumbs, pecans, and coconut until well mixed. Spread evenly over the graham crackers in pan. Top with another layer of graham crackers, cutting as needed and pressing down gently. Spread frosting over the top. Sprinkle with a few extra pecans, if you'd like.

Chill before cutting.

makes 24

Peanut Butter Mountain Bars

you'll need

¼ C. butter

2 C. creamy peanut butter

1 (11 oz.) pkg. butterscotch chips

2 (10 oz.) pkgs. mini marshmallows

to make

Coat a 9 x 13" pan with cooking spray; set aside.

In a medium saucepan, melt together butter and peanut butter. Add butterscotch chips, stirring constantly until melted. Remove from heat and let set for 10 minutes. Then pour into a large bowl with the marshmallows and stir. Spread evenly in prepared pan.

Refrigerate at least 1 hour before cutting.

Helpful Hint: Dump some peanuts in with the marshmallows if you'd like to add some crunch.

Cool Mint Oreo Squares

serves 9

you'll need

16 Cool Mint Oreo cookies

3 T. butter, softened

1 C. green mint chips

2 C. powdered sugar, sifted

½ (8 oz.) pkg. cream cheese, softened

¼ C. semi-sweet chocolate chips

Coat an 8 x 8" pan with cooking spray; set aside.

In a food processor, combine cookies and butter. Process until well blended. Press evenly into prepared pan and chill for 15 minutes.

Melt mint chips. Stir together melted chips, powdered sugar, and cream cheese until well blended. Spread evenly over chilled cookie layer.

Melt semi-sweet chocolate chips and drizzle over mint layer. Chill for 30 minutes before cutting.

Nutty Apricot Bars

makes 15

you'll need

- 1 (6 oz.) pkg. dried apricots
- 2 C. sweetened flaked coconut
- ¼ C. honey
- 8 oz. unsalted macadamia nuts
- ½ C. white baking chips, optional

Line a 7 x 11" pan with waxed paper, letting paper extend over two sides. Soak apricots in ¼ cup boiling water for 10 minutes to soften. Put coconut in a medium bowl. Set all aside.

Place apricots and soaking liquid in a food processor; add honey. Pulse until pureed but still slightly chunky. Add nuts and pulse to desired consistency. Transfer to the bowl with coconut; stir until well blended. Press mixture evenly into prepared pan and chill at least 1 hour before cutting.

Remove from pan by lifting the waxed paper. Melt white baking chips and drizzle over the bars, if desired.

makes 24

Saltine Toffee Treats

you'll need

24 saltine cracker squares

⅔ C. sugar

½ C. brown sugar

1 C. graham cracker crumbs

¼ C. milk

½ C. butter

½ C. dark chocolate chips

½ C. butterscotch chips

⅔ C. creamy peanut butter

Crushed mini M&Ms and
decorating sprinkles

to make

Coat a 9 x 13" pan with cooking spray.
Arrange crackers in the pan to cover
as much of the bottom as possible.

In a saucepan, combine sugar, brown
sugar, cracker crumbs, milk, and
butter. Bring to a full boil and boil for
5 minutes, stirring constantly. Remove
from heat. Slowly pour mixture over
crackers in pan. Set aside to cool.

Melt together chocolate chips,
butterscotch chips, and peanut
butter. Spread evenly over cooled
mixture. Scatter M&Ms and decorating
sprinkles over the top. Chill until set
before cutting.

23

serves 16

Chocolate Oaties

you'll need

1 C. butter

½ C. brown sugar

1 tsp. vanilla

3 C. quick-cooking oats

½ C. creamy peanut butter

½ C. dark chocolate chips

½ C. semi-sweet chocolate chips

to make

Spray a 9 x 9" pan with cooking spray and set aside.

In a medium saucepan, melt the butter. Add brown sugar and vanilla, stirring until well blended. Stir in the oats and cook several minutes until the mixture is hot and well blended. Press half the mixture into the bottom of the prepared pan; set aside the remainder.

Melt together the peanut butter and the dark and semi-sweet chocolate chips, stirring until smooth. Pour chocolate mixture over crust in pan, spreading evenly to cover. Crumble the set-aside mixture over the top, pressing gently.

Chill until chocolate is set before cutting.

Layered Java-Peppermint Cream

serves 12

you'll need

1¼ C. heavy cream

1 T. sugar

¼ C. coffee liqueur

6 ice cream sandwiches

10 hard peppermint candies, crushed

Beat cream and sugar until stiff peaks form; fold in coffee liqueur and beat until stiff peaks form again. Set aside.

Line a 5 x 9" loaf pan with parchment paper, letting paper extend over two sides. Arrange half the ice cream sandwiches in the pan crosswise to cover the bottom, cutting to fit as needed. Spread half the whipped cream over and around the sandwiches and sprinkle with half the candies. Arrange the remaining ice cream sandwiches over the candy and spread remaining whipped cream over and around them. Sprinkle with remaining candies. Freeze at least 4 hours.

Remove loaf from pan by lifting the parchment paper before slicing.

Nutterfinger Bites

makes 36

you'll need

- 1 (10 oz.) pkg. peanut butter chips
- 1 (14 oz.) can sweetened condensed milk
- 30 Nutter Butter cookies, finely crushed
- 2 (2.1 oz.) Butterfinger candy bars, coarsely chopped
- 36 Nutter Butter Bites cookies

Coat an 8 x 8" pan with cooking spray; set aside.

In a medium bowl, melt the peanut butter chips in the microwave, stirring until smooth. Stir in the sweetened condensed milk until well combined. Stir in crushed cookies and carefully fold in chopped candy bars. Spread evenly in prepared pan and arrange Nutter Butter Bites over the top, pressing gently.

Chill for 30 minutes before cutting.

makes 24

Trail Mix Cruncheroos

you'll need

- 2 (1 oz.) pkgs. pistachios, shelled
- ⅓ C. pure maple syrup
- 2 T. butter
- 4 C. mini marshmallows
- 1½ tsp. maple flavoring
- 1 (14 oz.) box Cranberry Almond Crunch cereal
- 1 C. dried cranberries

to make

Line a 9 x 13" pan with parchment paper, letting paper extend over two sides; spray paper with cooking spray. Chop pistachios. Set all aside.

In a large saucepan over medium heat, heat together syrup and butter until melted and bubbly. Add marshmallows, stirring until melted. Remove from heat and stir in maple flavoring, cereal, cranberries, and pistachios until everything is nicely coated. Transfer to the prepared pan and press down firmly.

Cool before cutting. Remove from pan by lifting the waxed paper.

Satin Pecan Bars

makes 16

you'll need

2 C. pitted dates, divided

3 C. chopped pecans, divided

3 T. peanut oil, divided

1 C. unsweetened flaked coconut

¾ tsp. salt, divided

2 T. pure maple syrup

½ C. dark chocolate chips, optional

Line an 8 x 8" pan with plastic wrap, letting plastic extend over two sides; set aside.

In a food processor, combine 1 cup dates, 1 cup pecans, 1 tablespoon oil, coconut, and ½ teaspoon salt. Process until well blended. Press evenly into prepared pan; chill for 30 minutes.

In the food processor, combine remaining 1 cup dates, syrup, remaining 2 tablespoons oil, 1 cup pecans, remaining ¼ teaspoon salt, and ¼ cup water. Process until thoroughly combined, scraping down sides of bowl as needed. Pour mixture over chilled crust, spreading evenly to cover. Sprinkle remaining 1 cup pecans over mixture in pan, pressing down gently. Melt chocolate chips and drizzle over the top, if you'd like.

Freeze overnight before cutting.

White Walnut Morsels

makes 36

you'll need

- 1 (14 oz.) can sweetened condensed milk
- 1 (12 oz.) pkg. white baking chips
- ½ C. chopped walnuts
- ½ tsp. vanilla
- 2½ C. graham cracker crumbs
- 1 oz. semi-sweet baking chocolate

Line an 8 x 8" pan with foil, letting foil extend over two sides. Coat with nonstick cooking spray; set aside.

In a large bowl, heat sweetened condensed milk and white baking chips together in the microwave until melted, stirring every 30 seconds. Stir in walnuts, vanilla, and cracker crumbs. Pour mixture into prepared pan, spreading evenly.

Chill until set before cutting. Melt baking chocolate and drizzle over bars.

Helpful Hint: Put melted chocolate in a small zippered plastic bag. Cut a tiny hole in the corner to drizzle chocolate.

serves 12

Banana Split Dessert

you'll need

⅔ C. halved maraschino cherries

1 (20 oz.) can pineapple tidbits, juice reserved

½ C. butter, melted

2 C. graham cracker crumbs

4 bananas

2 C. powdered sugar

1 C. butter, softened

½ (8 oz.) pkg. cream cheese, softened

1 (8 oz.) tub whipped topping, thawed

Chocolate decorating sprinkles, optional

to make

Set cherries and pineapple on layers of paper towels to drain. In a 9 x 13" pan, blend together melted butter and cracker crumbs; press evenly into the bottom of the pan. Slice the bananas about ½" thick and place in a bowl with the reserved pineapple juice; stir to coat. Set all aside.

Beat together powdered sugar, softened butter, and cream cheese until light and fluffy; spread evenly over graham cracker mixture in pan. Drain the bananas and place in a single layer over the cream cheese mixture. Cover with cherries and pineapple. Spread whipped topping evenly over the fruit. Chill for at least 2 hours.

Cut into squares and garnish each with decorating sprinkles. Top with a whole maraschino cherry, if desired.

Helpful Hint: *One package of nine graham crackers equals about 1½ cup of crumbs.*

makes 12

Creamy Caramel Crunch Bars

you'll need

Butter

4 to 5 whole graham crackers

1 (11 oz.) pkg. caramel bits

2 T. heavy cream

½ C. salted dry roasted peanuts

½ C. mini marshmallows

½ C. broken pretzels

¼ C. semi-sweet chocolate chips

to make

Line an 8 x 8" pan with foil, letting foil extend over two sides. Coat foil with butter. Arrange the crackers in the bottom of the pan, cutting to fit as needed; set aside.

Melt caramel bits with cream in the microwave for 2 minutes, stirring every 30 seconds until smooth. Pour over crackers in pan. Sprinkle with peanuts, marshmallows, and pretzels, pressing gently.

Melt the chocolate chips and drizzle over the mixture in the pan. Chill at least 1 hour.

Remove from pan by lifting the foil before cutting.

Peanut Butter Dots

In a saucepan, heat together ½ C. butter, ½ C. milk, and 2 C. sugar until melted. Bring to a boil; boil for 1 minute. Remove from heat. Add 1 tsp. vanilla, ½ C. creamy peanut butter, and a pinch of salt; stir until smooth. Stir in 3 C. quick-cooking oats and 1½ C. Reese's Pieces. Drop by spoonful onto waxed paper. Let set until firm.

makes 36

Sugared Mocha Balls

Beat ½ C. softened butter, ⅔ C. sugar, 3 T. unsweetened cocoa powder, 1 T. strong brewed coffee, and ½ tsp. vanilla until well mixed. Stir in 1¾ C. quick-cooking oats. Roll into 1" balls and roll in powdered sugar, if you'd like; place on waxed paper until firm.

makes 28

Classic No-Bakes

In a saucepan, heat together 2 C. sugar, ¼ C. unsweetened cocoa powder, ½ C. butter, and ½ C. milk until smooth and melted. Bring to a boil; boil for 1 minute. Remove from heat; stir in 1 C. peanut butter, 1 T. vanilla, and 3 C. quick-cooking oats. Drop by heaping tablespoonful onto waxed paper. Let set until firm.

makes 28

Almond Joys

Stir together 2 C. almond flour, 3 C. coconut, ½ C. softened butter, ½ C. honey, 2 C. semi-sweet chocolate chips, 1 tsp. vanilla, ½ tsp. coarse salt, and ¼ tsp. almond extract until well blended. Form into 2" balls, flatten slightly, and roll in additional coconut. Set on a waxed paper-lined tray and refrigerate until firm. Keep cookies stored in the refrigerator.

makes 24

Circus Bars

makes 18

you'll need

1 (3.2 oz.) pkg. microwave butter-flavored popcorn, popped (about 9 C.)

1 C. salted dry roasted peanuts

1 C. broken pretzels

1 C. light corn syrup

¼ C. butter

1 (11 oz.) pkg. butterscotch chips

1 C. plain M&Ms

Coat a 9 x 13" pan with cooking spray. Put popcorn, peanuts, and pretzels in a large bowl. Set aside.

In a medium saucepan, heat syrup and butter over medium heat until butter is melted. Bring to a full boil and boil for 1 minute, stirring constantly. Remove from heat and add the butterscotch chips, stirring until melted; pour over the popcorn mixture and stir until well coated. Stir in the M&Ms. Press the mixture evenly into prepared pan.

Chill for 1 hour before cutting.

Double Whammies

makes 24

you'll need

- 1 (9 oz.) pkg. chocolate wafers
- 1½ C. old-fashioned oats
- 1¼ C. powdered sugar
- ¼ tsp. coarse salt
- ½ C. plus 2 T. butter
- 1 C. crunchy peanut butter
- ¾ C. creamy peanut butter
- 1 (12 oz.) pkg. semi-sweet chocolate chips

Coat a 9 x 13" pan with cooking spray; line with parchment paper, letting paper extend over two sides and spray again. Set aside.

Crush the wafers and put into a large bowl. Stir in oats, powdered sugar, and salt. Melt together butter and all the peanut butter; stir into the crumb mixture. Press firmly into prepared pan. Chill for 30 minutes.

Melt the chocolate chips and pour evenly over chilled mixture, spreading to cover. Chill until chocolate has hardened.

Let set at room temperature 15 to 20 minutes and remove from pan by lifting the parchment paper before cutting.

serves 16

Icy Lemon-
Lime Minis

you'll need

- ¾ C. plus 2 T. graham cracker crumbs
- 1 T. plus 1 tsp. sugar
- 3 T. plus 2 tsp. butter, melted
- 1 pt. lime sherbet, softened
- 1 pt. lemon sorbet, softened
- 1 pt. vanilla frozen yogurt, softened
- 1 T. key lime juice
- Whipped topping, thawed

to make

Line 16 muffin cups with foil liners; set aside.

Stir together cracker crumbs, sugar, and butter; divide evenly among muffin cups and press down firmly. Set in the freezer for 15 minutes.

Combine sherbet, sorbet, and frozen yogurt; add lime juice and stir until well blended. Spoon mixture evenly onto crusts and press down firmly, filling liners. Freeze for several hours until firm.

Add a dollop of whipped topping. Garnish with a lime slice if you'd like. Serve immediately.

Easy Peanut Butter Bars

serves 15

you'll need

- 1 C. butter, melted
- 2 C. vanilla wafer crumbs
- 2 C. powdered sugar
- 1¾ C. creamy peanut butter, divided
- 1 C. semi-sweet chocolate chips
- 1 C. dark chocolate chips

Beat together butter, wafer crumbs, powdered sugar, and 1½ cups peanut butter. Spread evenly in a 9 x 13" pan.

Melt together all chocolate chips and remaining ¼ cup peanut butter; spread evenly over peanut butter layer.

Chill at least 1 hour before cutting.

Disappearing Ritz Bitz

serves 8

you'll need

- 1¼ C. marshmallow creme
- ½ C. crunchy peanut butter
- ¾ C. creamy peanut butter
- 36 Ritz crackers, coarsely chopped
- ¾ C. mini semi-sweet chocolate chips
- 1 oz. semi-sweet baking chocolate

Coat an 8 x 8" pan with cooking spray; set aside.

In a large bowl, mix marshmallow creme and all the peanut butter until well blended. Stir in crackers and chocolate chips. Press lightly into prepared pan.

Melt baking chocolate and drizzle over mixture in pan.

Let set for 30 minutes before cutting.

makes 24

Temptation S'mores Bars

you'll need

- ½ C. plus 2 T. butter, melted
- 2 C. powdered sugar
- ½ C. crunchy peanut butter
- ¾ C. creamy peanut butter
- 2 C. graham cracker crumbs
- 1 (7 oz.) container marshmallow creme
- 1 (12 oz.) pkg. milk chocolate chips
- 1 (12 oz.) pkg. mini peanut butter cups, coarsely chopped

to make

Coat a 9 x 13" pan with cooking spray; set aside.

In a bowl, combine butter, powdered sugar, all the peanut butter, and cracker crumbs; stir until well blended. Press into prepared pan. Spread the marshmallow creme evenly over dough.

Melt the chocolate chips and pour over the marshmallow layer, spreading evenly. Sprinkle the peanut butter cup pieces over the top.

Chill until the chocolate layer is set before cutting.

makes 16

Mocha Nanaimo Bars

you'll need

¾ C. sweetened flaked coconut

¾ C. finely chopped almonds

⅔ C. plus ¼ C. plus 2 T. butter, divided

⅓ C. unsweetened cocoa powder

¼ C. plus 1 tsp. sugar, divided

2 T. instant coffee or espresso powder, divided

1 egg, beaten

1½ C. graham cracker crumbs

2 C. powdered sugar

2 T. milk

3 oz. semi-sweet baking chocolate, chopped

to make

Line an 8 x 8" pan with parchment paper, letting paper extend over two sides. In separate skillets, toast coconut and almonds over medium heat for several minutes until golden brown, stirring occasionally. Set all aside.

In a medium saucepan, combine ⅔ cup butter, cocoa powder, ¼ cup sugar, 1 tablespoon coffee, and egg. Cook over low heat until butter is melted. Then cook 5 minutes more or until mixture starts to thicken, whisking constantly. Remove from heat. Stir in cracker crumbs, coconut, and almonds, stirring until well combined. Press evenly into prepared pan. Chill for 30 minutes.

In a bowl, beat powdered sugar, ¼ cup softened butter, and milk until smooth and creamy. Spread evenly over chilled mixture. Chill again for 1 hour.

Heat together remaining 2 tablespoons butter, remaining 1 tablespoon coffee, baking chocolate, and remaining 1 teaspoon sugar until melted, stirring until smooth; cool slightly. Pour over chilled mixture, spreading evenly to cover. Freeze until firm.

Cut into bars then remove from pan by lifting the parchment paper. Top with almonds, if you'd like.

Helpful Hint: *After mixture has been in the freezer for 4 or 5 minutes, score the chocolate with a sharp knife. Then return to freezer until firm.*

Lemon Delish

serves 15

you'll need

- 1 C. graham cracker crumbs
- ¾ C. plus 2 T. coarsely ground walnuts
- ½ C. butter, softened
- 1 (8 oz.) pkg. cream cheese, softened
- 1 C. powdered sugar
- 1 (8 oz.) tub whipped topping, thawed, divided
- 2 (3.4 oz.) pkgs. lemon instant pudding
- 3 C. milk
- ½ C. chopped walnuts

Coat a 9 x 13" pan with cooking spray. Stir together cracker crumbs, ground walnuts, and butter until thoroughly incorporated. Press firmly into prepared pan; chill.

In a medium bowl, beat together cream cheese and powdered sugar until well blended and smooth. Fold in half the whipped topping. Spread evenly over chilled crust; set aside.

In a separate bowl, beat pudding with milk for 2 minutes or until mixture just starts to thicken. Spread evenly over cream cheese layer. Chill until set.

Spread remaining whipped topping over the pudding layer and sprinkle with chopped walnuts.

Chill for 1 hour before cutting.

Salted Peanut Goodies

makes 20

you'll need

2 (8 oz.) pkgs. salted peanuts, divided

2 T. plus 1½ tsp. butter

1 (10 oz.) pkg. peanut butter chips

1 (14 oz.) can sweetened condensed milk

2 C. mini marshmallows

Coarse salt, optional

Scatter one package of peanuts evenly over the bottom of an ungreased 7 x 11" pan; set aside.

In a medium saucepan over low heat, melt together butter and peanut butter chips until nearly melted. Stir in sweetened condensed milk and marshmallows, stirring constantly until marshmallows are partially melted. Carefully spread mixture over peanuts. Sprinkle the remaining package of peanuts over the top; press down gently. Sprinkle with a little salt, if you'd like.

Refrigerate about 1 hour before cutting.

Helpful Hint: Coat a rubber spatula with cooking spray before using it to spread marshmallow mixture over peanuts.

makes 38

Confetti Cake Balls

you'll need

- ½ C. butter, softened
- ½ C. sugar
- 1 C. vanilla cake mix (or flavor of your choice)
- 1½ C. flour
- ⅛ tsp. salt
- 2 tsp. vanilla
- ¼ C. milk
- 2 T. decorating sprinkles, plus more for the top
- 8 squares almond bark

to make

Line a baking sheet with parchment paper and coat a wire rack with cooking spray; set aside.

In a large bowl, mix butter and sugar until well combined. Beat in cake mix, flour, salt, and vanilla. Add milk and blend until it becomes a dough-like consistency. Stir in 2 tablespoons decorating sprinkles. Roll into 1" balls and set on prepared baking sheet. Chill for 15 minutes.

Melt almond bark according to package instructions; stir until smooth. Using a fork or skewer, dip each ball into melted bark; remove, letting excess drip off. Set on prepared rack and scatter additional sprinkles on top. Continue with remaining balls.

Chill until coating is dry.

No-Bake Brownie Bites

makes 16

you'll need

¼ C. finely chopped almonds

1 C. graham cracker crumbs

½ tsp. coarse salt

¼ C. unsweetened cocoa powder

¾ C. sweetened condensed milk

1 (4 oz.) pkg. bittersweet baking chocolate, melted

Line an 8 x 8" pan with parchment paper; coat with cooking spray. Set aside. In a skillet, toast almonds over medium heat for several minutes until golden brown, stirring occasionally. Set aside.

In a medium bowl, mix cracker crumbs and salt. Stir in toasted nuts, cocoa powder, sweetened condensed milk, and melted chocolate until well blended. Press mixture evenly into prepared pan.

Chill for 1 hour before cutting.

M&M Cheerio Bars

makes 15

you'll need

- 3 T. butter
- 1 (10 oz.) pkg. mini marshmallows
- ½ C. creamy peanut butter
- 5 C. Cheerios cereal
- 1 C. regular M&Ms

Coat a 9 x 13" pan with cooking spray; set aside.

In a large bowl, microwave butter and marshmallows together until melted, stirring until smooth. Stir in the peanut butter until well blended. Fold in cereal and M&Ms until well coated. Press mixture evenly into prepared pan.

Cool slightly before cutting.

serves 36

Neapolitan Krispies

you'll need

9 T. butter, divided

2 (10 oz.) pkgs. regular marshmallows, divided

11 C. Rice Krispies cereal, divided

6 C. Cocoa Krispies cereal

1 (8 oz.) pkg. strawberry marshmallows

to make

Line a deep straight-edged 9 x 13" pan with foil, letting foil extend over two sides; coat with cooking spray and set aside.

Melt 3 tablespoons butter in a large saucepan over medium-low heat. Add one package regular marshmallows, stirring until melted and smooth. Remove from heat and stir in 6 cups Rice Krispies until evenly coated. Transfer to prepared pan. Using a rubber spatula coated with cooking spray, press mixture firmly into pan. Set aside.

In a clean saucepan, melt 3 tablespoons butter. Add remaining package of regular marshmallows and stir until melted. Stir in Cocoa Krispies until evenly coated. Press mixture firmly over plain layer in pan. Set aside.

Melt remaining 3 tablespoons butter in a clean saucepan. Add strawberry marshmallows, stirring until melted. Stir in remaining 5 cups Rice Krispies and press firmly over cocoa layer. Refrigerate until chilled.

Invert pan onto a cutting board to remove cereal; remove foil and cut.

serves 8

Mile-High
Berry Tiramisu

you'll need

3 C. chopped fresh strawberries

Juice from 1½ lemons

3 T. sugar

2 C. heavy cream

2 tsp. clear vanilla

½ C. powdered sugar

1 (8 oz.) container mascarpone cheese

14 ladyfingers

to make

Line a 5 x 9" loaf pan with plastic wrap, letting wrap extend over two sides. Combine strawberries, lemon juice, and sugar in a bowl; toss to coat. Set aside.

In a medium bowl, beat together cream, vanilla, and powdered sugar until soft peaks form. Add mascarpone cheese and beat until thick and creamy. Spread about ⅓ of the mixture in prepared pan and smooth the top. Arrange half the ladyfingers in a single layer over the top. Scatter half the strawberries evenly over the ladyfingers. Repeat layers. Spread remaining cream mixture evenly over the top. Cover and refrigerate several hours.

Slice tiramisu and remove from pan by carefully lifting the plastic wrap. Garnish with strawberries, if desired.

Orange-Orange Orbs

In a food processor, finely crush 1 (12 oz.) pkg. vanilla wafers with ½ C. sliced almonds, ½ C. coconut, and ½ C. powdered sugar. In a saucepan, heat together 1 C. white baking chips, 1 T. butter, ¼ C. orange juice, ¼ C. orange marmalade, and 2 T. light corn syrup until melted; stir until smooth. Stir in 1 tsp. orange flavoring. Mix crumb mixture with orange mixture. Form into 1½" balls, roll in additional powdered sugar, and set on waxed paper until firm.

makes 42

Criss-Cross Cookies

Mix 1¼ C. graham cracker crumbs, ½ C. creamy peanut butter, ⅓ C. light corn syrup, 1 tsp. vanilla, ¼ C. sugar, ½ tsp. cinnamon, and a pinch of ginger until well blended. (If the dough is too crumbly, add 2 to 3 T. more peanut butter). Form into 1" balls and set on a waxed paper-lined tray; flatten slightly with a fork in a criss-cross pattern. Melt 1 chocolate almond bark square; dip bottoms of cookies in chocolate or drizzle chocolate over the tops. Chill until set.

makes 20

Holly Jolly Cookies

In a saucepan, heat together ⅓ C. butter and 30 regular marshmallows until melted, stirring constantly. Remove from heat and stir in green food coloring to desired shade. Stir in 3 C. Corn Flakes cereal until evenly coated. Make mounds about 2½" in diameter on waxed paper coated with cooking spray. Press cinnamon candies into the top of each. Let set until firm.

makes 16

Cranberry-Nut No-Bakes

In a saucepan, heat together 1 (4 oz.) white chocolate baking bar (chopped) and 1 T. shortening until melted. Stir in 1½ C. coarsely chopped filberts and ⅓ C. dried cranberries. Let set for 10 minutes; drop by rounded tablespoonful onto waxed paper. Let set until firm. Drizzle with melted white chocolate, if you'd like.

makes 14

Sweet-Tart Gems

makes 16

you'll need

1½ C. crushed sugar cookies

⅔ C. butter, softened, divided

3 limes, divided

2 C. powdered sugar

Stir together crushed cookies and ⅓ cup butter until well blended. Press mixture evenly into an 8 x 8" pan. Zest and juice two of the limes. Set all aside.

Beat together powdered sugar, remaining ⅓ cup butter, lime zest, and 3 tablespoons lime juice until light and fluffy, scraping down the side of the bowl as needed. Spread evenly over crust in pan. Using a sharp knife, score the mixture into squares. Cut four ¼" slices from the remaining lime and cut each slice into four even pieces. Place one lime piece on each scored square. Discard remaining lime juice and lime or save for another use.

Chill for 1 hour before cutting along score lines.

Happy Birthday Bars

you'll need

- 1 (12 oz.) pkg. white baking chips
- 1 (15.25 oz.) pkg. Birthday Cake Golden Oreos
- 1 (14 oz.) can sweetened condensed milk
- 2 tsp. decorating sprinkles

Coat an 8 x 8" pan with cooking spray. Set aside ¼ cup baking chips and five Oreos; coarsely crush remaining Oreos.

In a medium saucepan, melt remaining baking chips, stirring until smooth; stir in sweetened condensed milk until well mixed. Add crushed Oreos, stirring until well coated; press mixture into prepared pan. Let set 5 minutes.

Crush remaining five Oreos and scatter over the top of the mixture in the pan. Top with decorating sprinkles and set-aside baking chips, pressing down lightly.

Chill for 1 hour before cutting.

serves 18

Caramel Apple Icebox Dessert

you'll need

About 16 whole graham crackers

5 cooking apples (such as Braeburn or Jonathan), peeled, thinly sliced

2 T. lemon juice

2 T. flour

½ C. brown sugar

2 tsp. ground cinnamon, divided

¼ tsp. ground nutmeg

1 (8 oz.) pkg. cream cheese, softened

½ C. powdered sugar

½ tsp. vanilla

2 T. caramel sauce

2 (8 oz.) tubs whipped topping, thawed, divided

1 C. milk chocolate toffee bits

to make

Cover the bottom of a 9 x 13" pan with a layer of graham crackers, breaking to fit as needed; set aside.

In the microwave, cook together apples, lemon juice, flour, brown sugar, 1 teaspoon cinnamon, and nutmeg for 8 to 10 minutes or until mixture has thickened and apples are soft, stirring occasionally. Cool completely.

In a large bowl, beat cream cheese until fluffy. Mix in powdered sugar and remaining 1 teaspoon cinnamon. Add vanilla and caramel sauce, beating until well blended. Fold in one tub whipped topping and spread half this mixture over the crackers in the pan. Carefully spread half the cooled apple mixture over the cream cheese mixture. Cover with half the remaining tub of whipped topping and sprinkle with half the toffee bits. Add another layer of crackers. Repeat layers, using the remaining cream cheese mixture, remaining apple mixture, remaining whipped topping, and remaining toffee bits. Crush any remaining cracker pieces and sprinkle over the top, if desired.

Chill for 1 hour before cutting.

Helpful Hint: These are best eaten the same day they're made.

63

Index